Greek Americans

SPIRIT
of America®

Greek AMERICANS

By Cynthia Klingel

*Content Adviser: Dr. George Kouvetaris, Professor of Sociology,
Northern Illinois University, DeKalb, Illinois*

The
**Child's
World**®

The Child's World®
Chanhassen, Minnesota

7

Greek AMERICANS

Published in the United States of America by The Child's World®
PO Box 326 • Chanhassen, MN 55317-0326 • 800-599-READ • www.childsworld.com

Acknowledgments
The Child's World®: Mary Berendes, Publishing Director

For Editorial Directions, Inc.: E. Russell Primm, Editorial Director; Sarah E. De Capua and Pam Rosenberg, Line Editors; Elizabeth K. Martin, Assistant Editor; Olivia Nellums, Editorial Assistant; Susan Hindman, Copy Editor; Joanne Mattern, Proofreader; Matthew Messbarger, Ann Grau Duvall, and Deborah Grahame, Fact Checkers; Tim Griffin/IndexServ, Indexer; Cian Loughlin O'Day, Photo Researcher; Linda S. Koutris, Photo Selector

Photos
Cover/frontispiece: University of Minnesota, Immigration History Research Center

Cover photographs ©: Sheldan Collins/Corbis

Interior photographs ©: Bettmann/Corbis: 12, 26; Corbis: 7 (James Davis; Eye Ubiquitous), 8 (Stapleton Collection), 9, 11 (Kevin Fleming), 14 (Richard Klune), 17 (Kelly/Mooney Photography), 19 (Nik Wheeler), 20 (Layne Kennedy), 21 (Gail Mooney), 23-top, 23-bottom (Arte & Immagini srl), 24 (Peter M. Wilson), 25 (Wally McNamee), 27 (AFP), 28 (Annie Griffiths Belt); Getty Images/Hulton Archive: 6, 10; University of Minnesota, Immigration History Research Center: 13, 15, 16, 22.

Registration
The Child's World®, Spirit of America®, and their associated logos are the sole property and registered trademarks of The Child's World®.

Library of Congress Cataloging-in-Publication Data
Klingel, Cynthia Fitterer.
  Greek Americans / by Cynthia A. Klingel.
    p. cm. — (Our cultural heritage)
"Spirit of America."
Includes bibliographical references (p.) and index.
Contents: Life in Greece—Adjusting to a new land—Greek-Americans
today—Influencing American culture.
  ISBN 1-59296-014-6 (lib. bdg. : alk. paper)
  1. Greek Americans—Juvenile literature. [1. Greek Americans.]
  I. Title. II. Series.
  E184.G7K55 2004
  973'.0489—dc21
                          2003004287

12   19   26

Contents

Jan. 2004 Davidson 14.00 Town

Chapter ONE

Life in Greece

FOR HUNDREDS OF YEARS, PEOPLE IN OTHER countries have thought of America as a land of opportunity. As a result, people from all over the world have moved to America in search of a better life. They have been immigrating from some countries for as long as 400 years and from others for fewer than 100 years.

Though a few Greeks arrived in the United States before 1900, most Greeks came to America in the 20th century. To understand why people from Greece left their homes, it is helpful to know a little bit about Greece. Greece is a

A Greek family wearing traditional Greek clothing

peninsula that reaches into the sea. It has a long, jagged coastline and rugged, rocky mountains. There is little land for farming. Long ago, the best way to travel around Greece was by sea. The Greeks were excellent sailors.

The coastline of Greece is long and rugged.

Ancient Greece was a strong and successful country. But it did not have enough land for all its people to live. There wasn't enough land to grow food. So the rulers of Greece encouraged people to immigrate to nearby places. After many years, powerful Greek leaders controlled a very large area. Many present-day countries were once a part of Greece.

In 1453, the Greeks lost control of these lands. For nearly 400 years afterward, the Greek people were ruled by Ottoman Turks. Living conditions were poor. The country fell into ruin. In 1821, the Greek war for **independence** began.

The people of America valued the Greeks and their culture. Many Americans went to

Interesting Fact

▶ The first Greek to set foot on American soil was sailor Don Theodoros. He was on a 1528 expedition with the explorer Narvaez.

The Greeks fought for their independence from the Turks in this battle at the Alamana Bridge.

Greece to help them in their fight. These Americans began helping some of the Greek people go to America. Most of these immigrants were Greek children—young men, **orphans,** and **refugees.** Some immigrants were sponsored by missionaries. In America, they would be able to get an education.

The Greeks won the war for their independence from the Turks in 1829, but only a small portion of their lands was liberated. Although life was still hard, most Greeks did not want to leave their homeland to live in America. They wanted to stay and help rebuild the country and the culture they loved. In 1848, only one Greek immigrant arrived in the port of New York. During that same year, 100,000 immigrants arrived from Ireland, and 50,000 from Germany. It is estimated that fewer than 200 Greek immigrants arrived in America from 1820 to 1870.

At first, Greece's new leaders were not strong. Over time, though, life improved, especially in the cities. For people living outside the cities, life was hard. Taxes were high. Wages were low. Earthquakes and **droughts** were constant threats.

Many Greeks didn't know how to solve these problems. Survival became more difficult. Finally, they began to leave for America. Between 1871 and 1880, 210 Greek immigrants arrived in America. Between 1880 and 1890, there were 2,308. Most of these immigrants were male, and many were from the area around Sparta.

In 1890, Greece suffered a serious drought and many farmers found it almost impossible to make a living.

In 1890, there was a serious drought in Greece. It was nearly impossible to grow crops. The people of rural Greece believed their only choice was to leave their country. Some Greeks moved to nearby countries, where their ancestors had moved hundreds of years before. But during the next ten years, almost 16,000 Greeks—mostly men—decided to sail to America.

Most of these men did not plan to live in America for long. Some of them left wives and children behind. They planned to make

9

▶ *Hellenes* is a Greek word meaning "Greek people." *Philhellenes* means "people who love the Greek culture and people." This term has often been used to describe Americans who appreciate Greeks and their culture.

In the early 1900s, all Greek men were required to serve in the military. These Greek soldiers are lined up and ready for inspection.

money, send it home to their families, and then return to Greece.

Between 1901 and 1910, 167,519 Greek immigrants arrived in the United States. Between 1911 and 1920, a record number of 184,201 arrived. Some of the reasons they came were the same as for those who had come before. Most immigrants left for economic reasons, though a few left Greece to avoid the military service. A law in Greece forced every Greek man to serve in the military.

After 1930, fewer Greek immigrants arrived in the United States. America's immigration laws changed. For a time, fewer people were allowed to immigrate.

Today's immigrants from Greece are well educated. Many of them are students in American colleges and universities. Some return to Greece, but others stay in the United States when they are finished with their education. There are thousands of Greek-American professionals, such as lawyers and teachers.

BEFORE THE LATE 1800S, FEW GREEKS CAME TO THE UNITED STATES. BUT there was one group of Greeks who arrived in America as early as 1768. A Scottish doctor named Andrew Turnbull had received permission to farm

20,000 acres (8,100 hectares) in Florida. He needed help and decided the hard-working people of Greece would make good farmhands. He knew that life in Greece was hard for many people at that time. He thought he could convince them to leave. So he went to Greece and promised people many things if they would go with him to America to work. Turnbull was not truthful about what life would be like for them.

About 1,400 people from Europe, including hundreds of Greeks, followed him to the town of New Smyrna, Florida. (Turnbull had named the town after the area of Smyrna, Greece, where his wife had lived.) When they arrived, it was nothing like Turnbull had described. It was not a beautiful paradise. It was a swamp filled with mosquitoes. There were no fruit trees full of olives. The workers were not paid well and did not receive any land of their own. They were treated cruelly by Turnbull and the other people who were in charge. Turnbull would not allow anyone to leave.

Many Greeks died trying to escape from New Smyrna. Others died because of the poor living conditions, hard work, and sickness. Finally, some escaped and got help from the Florida government. The remaining Greeks were freed. New Smyrna was deserted by 1776.

Chapter Two

Adjusting to a New Land

A Greek family arriving at Ellis Island in New York in 1925

BETWEEN 1821 AND 1934, 10 PERCENT OF THE Greek population arrived in America. Some of them had a friend or family member they could contact when they arrived. But many did not. As for all immigrants, life in a new land brought many problems.

The biggest problem was not knowing English. Even though many English words come from ancient Greek, the languages of Greek and English are very different. Because of this, it was even harder for these immigrants to learn English than it was for many of the other immigrant groups. It kept them from learning about the

American culture and the way things were done. New immigrants from Greece and other countries in southern Europe even encountered discrimination and hostility from other immigrants who had arrived in America earlier.

Because many of the Greek immigrants who arrived before 1920 didn't plan to stay in America, they didn't try to learn about the culture. They kept their Greek traditions and language. This kept them from becoming **"Americanized."** They were seen as different and sometimes treated badly. They could not live in certain sections of some cities. They could not go to many of the same places other people did. Unfortunately, this kind of treatment was not unusual at this time. Many other groups were treated in the same way.

These early Greek immigrants wanted to get jobs and make money so they could send

Members of a Greek-American organization posing for a picture. Like many other new immigrants to the United States, the Greeks tended to socialize with other Greek immigrants like themselves.

Interesting Fact

▶ Areas in Greece where families had relatives in America became prosperous because of the money that was sent to them.

it home. They did not buy land. Although most of them were farmers from the rural areas of Greece, they had to take jobs in factories. Some worked as fishers in New England, Florida, and California.

A fisher working on his boat in Greece. Some Greeks who immigrated to the United States made a living as fishers in New England, Florida, and California.

Others sold flowers, fruits, and candies on the streets of big cities. Many went west and worked in mines or helped to build the railroads. These were very difficult jobs. The immigrants had to work up to ten hours a day. These jobs did not pay a lot of money. No matter how little money the immigrants made, however, they sent it home to their families in Greece.

These Greek immigrants, who were almost all men, were often lonely. But most did not try to meet American women because they wanted to marry Greek women. Even if

14

they wanted to, it was difficult for them to meet Americans because of differences in language and culture. Many of the immigrants returned to Greece. Some of them had made enough money and then felt it was time to leave.

Many of the Greek immigrants who arrived in the United States after the 1920s planned to live permanently in America. They arranged for Greek women to come to America as their brides. The men relied on relatives and pictures to arrange these marriages. This made a difference in Greek life in America. The women brought with them the traditions and culture of Greece.

As Greek families settled in cities, they began to establish Greek churches and communities. Greeks formed

Holy Trinity Church is a Greek Orthodox church in the city of Holyoke, Massachusetts.

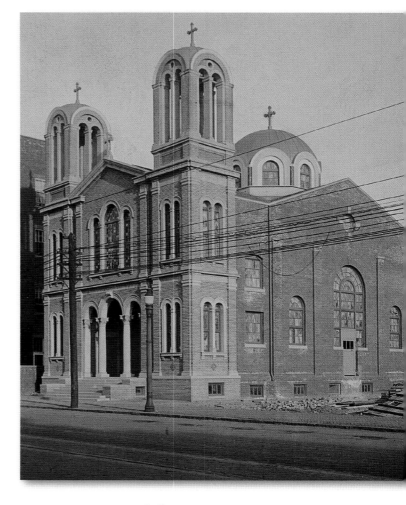

15

cultural organizations and societies. These groups planned social events, helped members solve problems, and helped to raise children in the Greek culture. In 1905, there were 100 Greek organizations in the United States.

Newspapers were also important. Many Greek newspapers were started. Printed in Greek, they gave the Greek Americans a way to learn about American life and customs. These papers helped the Greeks to become part of the American culture and also gave them information about current events in Greece.

The Greek Orthodox Church has always been an important part of Greek culture. The first thing members of a Greek community would do in America was build a church. This gave them the **roots** they needed to maintain their traditions and values. It gave them a place to meet and share their beliefs. It gave them an opportunity to teach their children about the meaning of being Greek.

Solon V. Vlasto was the publisher of the Greek-American newspaper Atlantis.

16

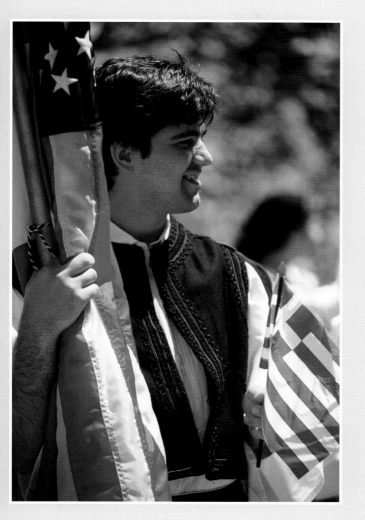

SOME GREEK IMMIGRANTS WHO arrived in the 1900s intended to live permanently in America. They had many challenges to overcome, however, to fit in and feel comfortable as Greek Americans.

In 1922, an organization was started to help Greeks become accepted citizens of America. This organization was called the American Hellenic Educational Progressive Association (AHEPA). Its official language was English, not Greek. The AHEPA wanted to change the negative image Americans had of Greek Americans. It focused on helping the immigrants become "Americanized."

But some of the Greek Americans believed the AHEPA was ignoring too many aspects of Greek culture. They thought that only American values and traditions were being accepted. They were afraid they were losing the very things they valued about being Greek.

So in 1923, they formed a new organization. It was called the Greek American Progressive Association (GAPA). Its goal was to preserve Greek heritage, language, and religious beliefs for Greek Americans. It was successful, but GAPA never became as big as AHEPA. GAPA no longer exists today.

Chapter THREE

Greek Americans Today

Interesting Fact

▶ Olympia Jean Snowe is the daughter of Greek immigrants. In 1978 she became the first Greek-American woman to be elected to the U.S. House of Representatives.

GREEK IMMIGRANTS ARRIVING IN AMERICA had many things in common. They settled in the same areas. There were certain jobs that most of them took. Their pay and living conditions were alike. They did not have a lot of places to go for entertainment. They didn't know a lot of other people.

Today, the circumstances are very different. Greek Americans vary from person to person. They don't live in the same places or work in similar jobs. Their incomes and living conditions vary from person to person.

In 2000, there were Greek Americans living in every state in the United States and in Washington, D.C. The state of New York is home to the most Greek Americans—159,763. North Dakota is home to only

18

about 600 Greeks—the least of any state. Most Greek Americans live in the Northeast. The Midwest is home to the second highest number. In recent years, many Greek Americans have moved to the warm Southern states. New York City, Chicago, and Los Angeles are the cities with the biggest populations of Greek Americans.

Greek Americans marching in a parade in Tarpon Springs, Florida

Greek Americans have different jobs than they did 100 years ago. Early Greek Americans worked at hard physical jobs, such as in mines in Utah, on the railroads, or in factories. Few Greek Americans work in difficult physical jobs now. Many Greek

▶ Some Greek immi-
grants settled in Tarpon
Springs, Florida, to
continue their trade of
sponge diving. Today,
the city is considered
the sponge capital of
the world.

*Greek food is served in
many restaurants in the
United States.*

immigrants were farmers and fishers in
Greece. Today, only a few Greek Americans
have chosen to work in agriculture or
fishing. More than half of today's Greek
Americans are professionals, such as doctors,
lawyers, and engineers.

Greek Americans have started successful
services. Many of these businesses are in the
restaurant industry. There are thousands of
successful Greek fast-food, family, and fine-
dining restaurants, coffee shops, and
catering services.
Greek Americans are
also prominent in the
movies, real estate, ice
cream parlors, fruit
stores, and many other
businesses.

Membership in
Greek societies is still
an important part of
life for Greek Ameri-
cans. As they have
become an accepted
part of American
culture, the need for

A traditional Greek folk dance

these societies has changed. Many of the older societies that helped the Greek immigrants face the problems of living in a new country no longer exist. Today's societies have a focus on supporting Greek culture and the Greek people living both in the United States and Greece.

Today's Greek youth and young adults are proud of their **heritage.** Few of the Greek

Americans change their Greek names to more American names as was once done. There is a strong interest in belonging to Greek churches and organizations. Greek Americans have become as individual as other Americans. But the Greek Orthodox Church and the Greek societies give the Greek Americans a strong connection to their culture.

Many young Greek Americans have an appreciation for the art of Greece, such as this religious painting.

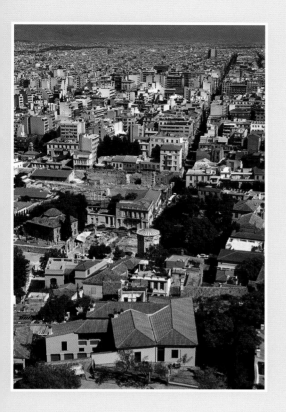

GREECE IS A COUNTRY ON THE COAST OF THE Mediterranean Sea. It is slightly smaller than the state of Alabama. It is made up of the Greek mainland and many large and small islands. Most of the country, including the islands, is mountainous.

Southern Greece has hot, dry summers and cool winters. Winters can be harsh in the mountains of northern Greece. The climate there is good for many rare plants and flowers.

The population in Greece is about 11 million. Only two percent of the population is made up of people who come from other countries. Greek is the official language, but many people also speak English and French. Most of the people belong to the Greek Orthodox Church.

Greece depends on shipping and tourism for much of its business. Some of the most visited places are the Acropolis in Athens; the Parthenon, a temple dedicated to Athena, the ancient goddess of wisdom; Mount Olympus, which is famous in Greek mythology as the home of the gods (pictured below); Delphi, the site of a shrine to Apollo; Corinth; Olympia, where the Olympic Games began; and Crete, an island that was home to the Minoans, the first civilization in Europe.

Chapter FOUR

Influencing American Culture

The Theater of Dionysos in Athens, Greece, is one example of ancient Greek architecture.

THE PEOPLE OF GREECE HAVE HAD GREAT accomplishments for thousands of years. We see this in Greek architecture, drama, literature, government, and art. Beauty and grace are elements of the Greek style. Many aspects of American life have roots in the Greek culture. This was true even before Greek immigrants settled in America. Since then, Greek Americans have made contributions to all areas of American culture.

The American founding fathers were fond of Greek culture and borrowed many

24

ideas from the ancient Greeks. One of the things Americans value most came from ancient Greece: our form of government. The word *democracy* is from a Greek word that means "the people rule." A democracy is a government that allows its people to choose their leaders.

Greek-American Spiro Agnew was elected vice president of the United States in 1968.

What do the words *alphabet, gymnasium,* and *symphony* have in common? They are all words that have come to us from the Greeks. Many English words have their roots in the Greek language.

Architecture, the way buildings are designed and built, is often modeled after the Greek style. One example is the Lincoln Memorial in Washington, D.C. Also, many American cities have the beautiful rounded **domes** of Greek Orthodox churches.

A number of Greek Americans have become important in American culture. There are many Greek Americans in politics. Spiro Agnew was elected vice president of the United States in 1968. Before that, he was the governor of Maryland. Former governor

Interesting Fact

▶ Actress Olympia Dukakis says that Greek Americans are known for their appetite for life.

25

Elia Kazan was a famous Greek-American movie director.

of Massachusetts Michael Dukakis was nominated by the Democrats to run for president in 1988. He lost to George H. W. Bush. The U.S. ambassador to the United Nations, John Negroponte, and the director of the CIA, George Tenet, are also Greek Americans. Another Greek American who played a role in politics and government is George Stephanopolous. He was an adviser to President Bill Clinton. Stephano-poulos now hosts a television news program.

Ancient Greece was the birthplace of the theater. Many Greek-American actors, direc-tors, and musicians have kept that tradition alive in the United States. Telly Savalas was well known as the bald-headed television character Kojak. Olympia Dukakis has worked as an actress, director, producer, and teacher. She won an Academy Award for her role in the movie *Moonstruck.* Elia Kazan is a Greek-American movie director. Maria Callas was a famous opera singer. One of the most popular independent films of all time is *My Big Fat Greek Wedding.* It cost about $5 million to produce, but made over $300 million worldwide! Nia Vardalos wrote and starred in the movie, which taught many people about Greek-American traditions and culture.

Greek Americans have excelled in many sports. One familiar Greek American is tennis player Pete Sampras. Sampras has become one of the best tennis players in the world, winning more major tournaments than any other male player.

Greek-American actress Nia Vardalos wrote and starred in the movie My Big Fat Greek Wedding.

The delicious smells of Greek food come from restaurants in any Greek neighborhood. Greek specialties include moussaka, made of eggplant, beef, and cream sauce, and spanakopita, a kind of spinach and feta cheese pie. Lamb roasted with herbs is an important food at Easter for those who are Greek Orthodox. Baklava is a tasty dessert treat made with phyllo dough, chopped nuts, and honey.

But you do not have to go to a Greek neighborhood to eat Greek food. Gyros have become very popular in the United States. The name comes from the Greek word meaning "to turn." To make a gyro, thin slices of meat are cut off a large piece of seasoned meat that has been turning and cooking on a spit. The meat is usually topped with tomatoes, onions, and a yogurt dip called tzatziki. It is all wrapped up in a flat bread called pita. Many American restaurants also serve Greek salad made of cucumbers, tomatoes, feta cheese, and herbs—no lettuce!

Greek Americans continue to find success and make contributions in their work, in their cities, and at the national level. American culture continues to benefit from the accomplishments of not only the Greeks who lived long ago, but also today's Greek Americans.

Greek-American women making traditional Greek pastries

Time LINE

1829   **1925**   **1968**

1453 Ottoman Turks take control of Greece.

1768 Scottish doctor Andrew Turnbull convinces hundreds of Greeks and other Europeans to move to New Smyrna in the present-day state of Florida to help farm his land. They are treated very poorly.

1821 The Greek war for independence begins.

1829 The Greeks win their war for independence from the Turks, but only a small amount of their land is liberated.

1848 One Greek immigrant arrives in the United States.

1820–1870 Less than 200 Greek immigrants arrive in the United States.

1871–1890 Greek immigrants to the United States number only 210.

1881–1890 Greek immigration to the United States increases, and 2,308 Greeks arrive in America.

1890 Greece experiences a drought, making life even more difficult for people living there.

1901–1910 167,519 Greek immigrants arrive in the United States.

1905 There are 100 Greek organizations helping Greek immigrants in the United States.

1911–1920 The number of Greek immigrants totals 184,201 during this period.

1922 The American Hellenic Educational Progressive Association (AHEPA) is founded.

1923 The Greek American Progressive Association (GAPA) is formed.

1968 Spiro Agnew is elected vice president of the United States.

1988 Michael Dukakis is nominated as the Democratic Party's candidate for president of the United States. He loses the election to George H. W. Bush.

2000 Greek Americans live in every state of the United States and Washington, D.C.

"Americanized" (ah-MARE-ih-kun-ized)
This means to become American in customs, speech, beliefs, and other characteristics. Because many immigrants kept their Greek traditions and language, they failed to become "Americanized."

catering (KAY-tur-ing)
Catering is providing food and service to others. There are thousands of successful Greek fast-food, family, and fine-dining restaurants, coffee shops, and catering businesses.

domes (DOHMZ)
A dome is a round roof shaped more or less like half a globe. Many American cities have the beautiful rounded domes of Greek Orthodox churches.

droughts (DROWTS)
A drought is a long period of dry weather, with little or no rain. In 1890, there was a serious drought in Greece.

heritage (HAIR-ih-tij)
Heritage is something that is handed down from one's ancestors or from the past, such as skills or traditions or a way of life. Its goal was to preserve Greek heritage, language, and religious beliefs for Greek Americans.

independence (in-dee-PEN-dens)
Independence is the freedom from the control of another. In 1821, the Greek war for independence began.

orphans (OR-funz)
Orphans are children whose parents are dead. Most early immigrants were Greek children—young men from wealthy families, orphans, and refugees.

refugees (REF-yoo-geez)
A refugee is someone who runs away from his or her country to seek protection from war or harsh treatment. Most early immigrants were Greek children—young men from wealthy families, orphans, and refugees.

roots (ROOTS)
Roots are the close ties that someone has with some place or people through birth, upbringing, or long association. Many aspects of American life have roots in Greek culture.

For Further INFORMATION

Web Sites

Visit our homepage for lots of links about Greek Americans:
http://www.childsworld.com/links.html

Note to Parents, Teachers, and Librarians:
We routinely verify our Web links to make sure they're safe,
active sites—so encourage your readers to check them out!

Books

Ferris, Julie. *Ancient Greece: A Guide to the Golden Age of Greece.* New York: Kingfisher, 1999.

Jones, Jayne Clark. *The Greeks in America.* Minneapolis: Lerner Publishing Group, 1990.

Monos, Dimitris. *The Greek Americans.* New York: Chelsea House, 1996.

Places to Visit or Contact

American Hellenic Educational Progressive Association
1909 Q Street, N.W.
Suite 500
Washington, DC 20009
202/232-6300

Hellenic Museum and Cultural Center
168 North Michigan Avenue
4th Floor
Chicago, IL 60601
312/726-1234

Index

About the Author

CYNTHIA KLINGEL HAS WORKED AS A HIGH SCHOOL English teacher and an elementary school teacher. She is currently the curriculum director for a Minnesota school district. Cynthia Klingel lives with her family in Mankato, Minnesota.